GRACE

The marvellous gift of God

SELWYN HUGHES

GRACE

The marvellous gift of God

Copyright © CWR 2004

First published by CWR as *Every Day with Jesus, The Pacesetters,*
January/February 2002.

Revised edition published 2004 by CWR as *The Scandal of Grace:
God's amazing gift.*

This edition reprinted 2005 by CWR, Waverley Abbey House,
Waverley Lane, Farnham, Surrey GU9 8EP, England.

The right of Selwyn Hughes to be identified as the author of this
work has been asserted by him in accordance with the Copyright,
Designs and Patents Act 1988, sections 77 and 78.

See back of book for list of National Distributors.

Unless otherwise indicated, all Scripture references are from the Holy
Bible: New International Version (NIV), copyright © 1973, 1978, 1984
by the International Bible Society.

Concept development, editing, design and production by CWR

Printed in Slovenia by Compass Press

ISBN 1-85345-368-4

CONTENTS

INTRODUCTION

Whatever else you may lack in the coming years, I can assure you in the name of Him who sits upon the throne that there is one thing you will not lack, and that is the gift of grace. No year has yet dawned that has not brought difficulties and problems. Indeed, if there were such a year it would be debilitating to the soul. Yet you can be sure that whatever happens in your life, grace will be there to sustain you and support you. You may run out of many things but you will never run out of grace.

One observation I have made is that Christians can be divided into two categories: those who appear to be thriving and those who are merely surviving. You must have noticed this yourself – some believers seem to travel faster along the path of Christian discipleship than others. We grow old at the same rate but we do not all seem to grow in the spiritual life at the same rate. Some people, even though they have been on the Christian pathway for 50 years or more, appear to have progressed at a snail's pace, while others have covered the same distance in five. Why is this? There are many possible answers but I am sure that one of the chief ones is this: they have appropriated for themselves what is described as 'God's abundant provision of grace' (Rom. 5:17). They have opened themselves to it and thus they stride along the Christian pathway at speed becoming 'pacesetters' – people who set the pace for others.

Has there been a slowing down in your spiritual life

lately? Have you slackened off spiritually? Then tell the Lord now you want to receive His gift and get back in the race again, moving forward with the most ardent believers you know.

CHAPTER ONE

GRACE ABUNDANT

Galatians 5:1–17

Acts 20:13–38

Genesis 17:1–8

'Now I commit you to God and to the word of
his grace, which can build you up …'
Acts 20:32

C an you imagine the disappointment Paul felt over some of the Galatian converts? 'You were running a good race,' he tells them. 'You were!' (Gal. 5:7). Paul had to use the past tense when speaking of their accomplishments.

Perhaps you turned aside from the question I asked in the introduction to this book: Has there been a slowing down in your spiritual life lately? Gently I ask you to face it again. Can it be said of you that you were running a good race but now you have slowed down? Once you pressed forward along the Christian pathway with zest and zeal. You responded to God's grace and it came in like the waves of the sea – one breaker after another. Yet maybe the moment came when God led you to some new task and you pulled away. You felt you couldn't go that far with Him, that the demands were too great. You forgot that God's finger never points the way without His hand providing the strength you need to accomplish the task He has for you. You didn't understand, as Romans 5:17 tells us, that God does not give His grace sparingly but in abundance. That means there is much more grace available than you will ever need. Was that when you began to slow down – when God challenged you to make some new form of surrender – the surrender of your time, money, service? You realise that people who started on the Christian pathway long after you have swept past you and are out ahead.

God needs all of you.

If this is your situation what are you going to do about

it? God needs all of you just as much as He ever did. Look back over your life right now to discover when you began to slow down. Then ask His forgiveness for your lack of keenness and decide to start moving again.

In time of need

Before going any further we must pause to define what we mean by 'grace'. Usually grace is defined as 'God's unmerited favour'. 'Grace,' says one writer, 'is shorthand for God's redeeming love.' Grace as undeserved favour is a concept that is still used in the business world. Companies sometimes say concerning a claim: 'We do not accept liability for this claim, but we will make an ex gratia [out of grace] payment.' They acknowledge no liability, but out of goodwill they make a token payment to which the person concerned has no legal right. And agreements sometimes contain a grace period in which one party freely gives another party time to rectify a fault.

Through God's grace we can face anything.

One person made this memorable comment: 'Grace always has a stoop in it. Love reaches out on the same level, but grace reaches down to pick us up.' The best definition of grace I have come across, though, is this: 'Grace is the strength God gives us which enables us to live or do as Jesus would do were He in our situation.' Simple, but sublime.

However, we should not think of grace merely as

unmerited favour or the loving kindness of God. It is important to recognise also that it is the inner strength He lends to men and women like ourselves who need a power other than their own to cope with the various issues and problems that life brings. You can be sure of this: the people who speed past us on the path of Christian discipleship have received more of the strength which God imparts. I don't think I am wrong when I say that nothing can happen in your life today for which divine strength will not be given. Through God's grace we can face anything that comes providing, of course, we avail ourselves of it.

Undistinguishing regard

Whenever I speak on the subject of grace from the pulpit I can almost guarantee that someone will come up to me afterwards and say: 'If grace is available to help each of us move along the Christian pathway at a steady pace then why is it that some people seem to possess more of this grace than I do?' Often I turn that question back on the questioner and respond: 'Why do you think that is so?' The answers that come are usually along this line: 'Because God favours some more than others.' Does God really have favourites? Is He like some men and women we may know who are biased in their affections and prefer one person to another? Surely not.

The thought that God takes a liking to one but not to another is preposterous. Look again at the verse that has been described as the greatest text in the Bible. What does it say? 'God so loved special people in His universe'? No. 'God so loved the world.' That means everyone. And why do we know it means everyone? Because 'whoever believes in him shall not perish' (John 3:16). No, a thousand times no, there is no favouritism on God's part when it comes to giving the gift of salvation, and there is no favouritism either when it comes to giving grace to those who stand in need.

Charles Wesley, the world's finest hymn writer, referred to grace as 'God's undistinguishing regard'. So be assured of this: if you are not receiving the grace you need in your life to leap over all the impediments on your onward way it is not because God is not as favourably disposed to you as He is to others. The problem is never God's unwillingness to give, it is always our unwillingness to receive.

Saved and sustained

During my life I have got to know hundreds of 'pacesetters', those who have set the pace for others. One of their characteristics is that they are people who know there is grace to be had. That is the crest and crown of it all.

Many Christians go through life relying on their own resources. Though they know in theory that God's strength is available to help them face anything that comes, in practice they do not draw upon it. Something that has surprised me greatly over the years is the number of Christians who go about as if God's dealings with them ended when they surrendered to Him. They talk about being saved by grace, but they seem to know nothing about being sustained by grace. Their spiritual talk is only of their conversion. God does not just call us to be saints – His grace is available to make us saints.

Those who accept this truth are conscious there is a power that far exceeds their own resources and that they do not have to stumble along the path of Christian discipleship unaided. Do you know someone who is younger than you in terms of discipleship yet demonstrates Christian qualities that you seem to struggle to put into effect – qualities such as an ability to forgive injuries, freedom from jealousy, lack of censoriousness, or joy when others do better at the things they themselves would like to do and praise them for it? And perhaps some of these people just a year or two ago were wallowing in sin! You can be sure of this: they are believers who live in constant awareness that God's grace is available to meet their every spiritual need.

His grace is available to make us saints.

'We talk abundance here'
Christians who set the pace for others are aware of texts such as the one I referred to in the introduction to this book which speaks of 'those who receive God's abundant provision of grace' (Rom. 5:17). You see, you will not be ready to receive God's grace unless you are convinced

that grace is available to help you get through every problem and difficulty.

You may think this is a simple point to make and that we ought now to move on, but I assure you there are multitudes of Christians who live as if their commitment to Jesus Christ was a completion rather than a commencement. They seem totally unaware of the fact that God's concern is not merely to impute righteousness to them (to regard them as sinless) but to impart it also. Conversion is not something rounded off but something just begun. God has more to give than saving grace and with this thought constantly in view they are kept from complacency. Always they are conscious that although they have already received much from the God of grace there is still far more to have.

Conversion is something just begun.

On the wall of an office in New York where major business deals are transacted there hangs a card which reads: 'We talk abundance here.' When Christians talk about the grace of God revealed in Jesus Christ, they should 'talk abundance'. As the old hymn so fittingly describes God's grace:

> *Its streams the whole creation reach,*
> *So plenteous is its store,*
> *Enough for all, enough for each,*
> *Enough for evermore.*

'The Enough'

The Hebrew name El Shaddai, which appears in our Bibles as 'God Almighty', can also be translated 'The Nourisher of His People'. One Bible teacher suggests that the English equivalent of El Shaddai is 'The Enough'. However we translate this name, it certainly conveys the fact that God's resources infinitely exceed our requirements. His sufficiency immeasurably surpasses every demand that we may make upon it. There is grace enough for everything – even the most heinous sin.

Has it ever occurred to you that only sinners can appreciate grace? One writer has made the comment that God may be said to love the angels, but He cannot be said to exercise grace towards them. It is sin, he says, that transforms love into grace.

Truly, to a believer, the message of grace is the sweetest sound it is possible to hear. Small wonder that when D.L. Moody, the American evangelist who preached in the nineteenth century, was meditating on the theme of grace, he was so captivated by the thought that, flinging aside his pen, he dashed out into the street where he accosted the first man he met and demanded: 'Do you know grace?' 'Grace who?' asked the surprised man.

In the words of Wesley's hymn:

> *Plenteous grace with Thee is found,*
> *Grace to cover all my sin.*
> *All!*

Further Study

2 Sam. 22:1–4; 22:17–33; Psa. 103:8–18; Luke 10:16–24;
Eph. 6:10–18

1. How does the psalmist portray God?
2. What obstacles can be overcome in the strength
   of God?

Gen. 45:1–15; Phil. 1:12–26

3. How did grace overcome sin in Joseph's life?
4. How does Paul demonstrate the grace of
   God in his life?

Gen. 28:1–5; 35:9–15; Psa. 103:1–5; 1 John 1:5–7

5. What promises did El Shaddai give to Jacob?
6. Of what promise does John assure his readers?

CHAPTER TWO

ASK

Psalm 42:1–11

James 4:1–3

1 John 5:13–21

*'As the deer pants for streams of water, so my
soul pants for you, O God.'*
Psalm 42:1

Not only is there sufficient grace to deal with our sin, there is grace for suffering too. 2 Corinthians 12:1–10 makes that abundantly clear.

Paul talks about having a thorn in the flesh. What was it? Some think it was ophthalmia. Others believe it was recurring malaria, or epilepsy. One commentator believes it to be a troublesome evil spirit that was allowed by God to harass the apostle and so keep him humble. Chrysostom, one of the Early Church Fathers, believed the 'messenger of Satan' was 'all the adversaries of the word … for they did Satan's business'. It is impossible for anyone to be sure exactly what Paul's thorn in the flesh was. One writer has wittily observed: 'Paul had a thorn in the flesh and nobody knows what it was; if we have a thorn in the flesh everybody knows what it is!' What we do know for certain is that Paul's thorn in the flesh was sufficiently distressing for him to plead with the Lord three times for it to be taken away. Yet it remained. And at last came the comforting word: 'My grace is sufficient for you, for my power is made perfect in weakness' (2 Cor. 12:9). I love the Living Bible paraphrase of this text that reads: 'My power shows up best in weak people.'

Take this truth to heart: there is grace not only to cover our sin but also to sustain us in times of suffering. Sufficient! Enough! Are you suffering at the moment? A sickness perhaps? Or harassment and persecution? God's grace was sufficient for the apostle in his suffering and it will be also for you.

What we can't do without

Grace comes in sufficient quantities from God to cover every sin, and also strengthens us to cope with every kind of suffering. But there's more – there's grace for service too.

Paul, in 1 Corinthians 15:1–11, is defending himself against his critics. Referring to the other apostles, he says: 'I worked harder than all of them' (v.10). At first this sounds like an arrogant boast. But he immediately qualifies it by saying: 'Yet not I, but the grace of God that was with me.' Believe me, you cannot go far in the realm of Christian service without that. So often our labours for Christ go unnoticed by others, or unappreciated, or unrewarded (in earthly terms, I mean). They may even be apparently unfruitful. Unless we are empowered by the grace of God then it is so easy to lose heart and give up. But there is no need for that situation to arise because He has grace – grace in abundance – to give to those who need it. If you allow Him, He will give you the patience and courage to press on. Then, when at last you come to the end of life's journey and look back upon a record of faithful toil, like the apostle Paul you will disclaim any entitlement to recognition or praise and say as he did: 'Yet not I, but the grace of God that was with me.'

There are many things we can do without in this world: we can do without wealth, we can do without social standing, we can do without a lengthy education, we can do without a large circle of friends, but we cannot do without grace. And God has enough for everyone.

Now the question remains: Is the thought that you don't have to muddle through on your own part of your conscious thinking? If not, then why not?

'I want nothing except ...'

Another characteristic I have observed in some Christians is this: they seek grace earnestly. They want it more than they want anything else.

Have you ever heard the name Fletcher of Madely? He was a great friend of John Wesley and the man whom Wesley designated as his successor in the leadership of the Methodist people, though as it turned out he died before Wesley. Fletcher once made an important public statement on an issue that was exercising the minds of many people at that time, and by so doing rendered a great service to the government of the day. The then Lord Chancellor dispatched an official to ask Fletcher if there was anything he wanted in return for the service he had done for the country. 'How very kind,' said Fletcher to the official when he delivered his message. 'But I want nothing except more grace.' Imagine the official returning to the Lord Chancellor and reporting: 'He doesn't want anything. There is nothing we have that appeals to him. He only wants more grace.'

> We must always look at the treasures of earth in the light of heaven.

We must always look at the treasures of earth in the

light of heaven. We should realise that the most valuable thing one can possess on this earth is grace, and want it ardently. 'Let me have that,' you will say, 'and I can handle anything that comes.' So it is not enough to know that grace is there or to keep it constantly in mind; we must want it more than we want anything else.

'Ask and it will be given'

Knowing God is a God of grace is not enough; we must want the grace He gives and want it ardently. We should desire to live by grace and desire it passionately.

An apocryphal story is told about a man who died and went to heaven. While he was being given a tour of the holy city he noticed an odd-looking building with no windows that appeared to be a warehouse. Having asked to see inside, he discovered that the whole building was filled from floor to ceiling with row after row of shelves. On them were thousands and thousands of boxes, each with a name written on it. After searching for the box bearing his own name, he opened it and found a list of all the things God wanted to give him while he was on earth – things he did not receive because he had never asked for them.

'Have you asked?'

James 4 verse 2 tells us: 'You do not have, because you do not ask God.' When Jesus was here on earth He said to His disciples: 'Ask and it will be given to you' (Matt. 7:7). But why should God withhold things from us simply because we do not ask? Isn't that being a little petulant? Surely, because God is loving and good, He can be expected to pour His blessings into our life irrespective of whether or not we ask. Asking is important for this reason: it tilts our soul in the direction of receiving. The very action of asking implies humility and a recognition of dependence on Another who alone can give us what we cannot provide for ourselves. Often when people have told me that they do not receive from God in the way others appear to do I have put this question to them: 'Have you asked?' Invariably they answer: 'No.' 'Then,' I say, 'why are you disappointed?'

Asking is not always selfish

If, as we have seen previously, there are many things we do not receive from God because we do not ask then why are we so reluctant to ask? On countless occasions Christians have told me that during their prayer times they never ask for things from God because, in their words: 'It seems so selfish.' They believe it is impolite to ask God for something for themselves or feel sure that God will consider them greedy if they ask for too many blessings. Some very earnest Christians regard it as a sign of spiritual immaturity to ever think in terms of asking for things for themselves. Of course, if our prayers are always geared to our own blessings and we are always asking for things for ourselves then most certainly it is a selfish form of praying.

I have always loved the story of the young unmarried woman who constantly prayed in the mid-week church prayer meeting for a husband. 'Lord, give me a husband,' she would say, and then sit down. Her vicar tried to help her towards spiritual maturity by saying: 'It's all right to pray for a husband, but you need to broaden your prayer life. Pray for other people as well as yourself.' So, in the next prayer meeting, she got up and prayed: 'Lord, please give my mother a son-in-law.'

Don't be afraid to ask Him for things.

Prayer that is always self-seeking and shot through with self-interest lacks maturity. Having said that, however, it is not wrong, when appropriate, to ask for things for yourself. Asking for grace to be poured into your life, for example, is not a self-centred request but a deeply spiritual one. It's exactly the kind of request your heavenly Father likes to hear. Don't let anything deter you from asking God for His grace to be given to you. Ask!

What you're supposed to feel

A clue as to why we have this basic disinclination to ask was given to me on one occasion when I put this question to a woman in counselling: 'Have you asked God to help you in this?' She replied: 'Asking makes me feel so dependent and helpless.' There's the rub. There is something about our carnal nature that abhors helplessness. We just don't like feeling dependent.

Bruce Wilkinson, an American writer, tells how he was faced with the situation of door after door bursting open in his ministry yet somehow being unable to shake off the feeling that he was not the man for the job. He sought counsel from a Bible teacher who had been a spiritual father to thousands. 'Son,' the godly man said, 'that feeling you are running from is called dependence. The second you are not feeling dependent you are not walking with the Lord Jesus.' Bruce replied: 'You're saying the feeling that I just can't do it is what I'm supposed to be feeling?'

For some this is a challenging truth, but as God's children we are to live in daily dependence upon Him. There are a number of things we can get for ourselves such as groceries from the supermarket, petrol from a garage, water from a tap, but there is one thing we cannot obtain for ourselves except by asking … and that is grace. The men and women of the world don't seem to set any great store by dependence, but the sons and daughters of God are to live by it. Though it may make us feel dependent and helpless to have to ask God for things, that's the way He has set it up. We need to know and accept that, and humbly put ourselves in the way of it by asking. So once again, don't try to struggle through on your own. Ask.

A prayer always answered

According to some research done by a group of young people in an American church, one of the least read books of the Bible is the first book of Chronicles. That's because the first nine chapters are taken up with the family tree of the Hebrew tribes, beginning with Adam and proceeding through long periods of time to Israel's return from captivity. This formidable list of names has made even the bravest of students turn back.

Yet, as with all difficult passages of Scripture, there are rewards for pressing through. And one of them is to come across this little known prayer of Jabez which consists of just twenty-nine words. Before it there are names, and after it there are names, but tucked away in between is this amazingly simple but powerful prayer. There was something about Jabez that caused the historian to pause. It is as if he is saying: 'Wait a minute. You need to know something about this man Jabez. He stands head and shoulders above the rest.' You can search the Bible and you will not find Jabez mentioned anywhere else. Clearly his prayer caught the attention of the writer of Chronicles: 'Oh, that you would bless me and enlarge my territory.' He was not being selfish in that prayer, he was simply asking for what he believed God wanted to give him. God is at work in our lives. Don't be afraid to ask Him for things, especially His grace. It's there for the asking – and the taking.

Was Jabez' prayer answered? Most definitely. When he asked, God heard his prayer. The following five words are some of the sweetest in the Bible: 'And God granted his request' (v.10). When you ask for needed grace be assured of this: your prayer will always be answered.

'Ask, man, ask'

To know that grace is there in abundance is one thing, but to ask for it is another. The story is told of a man who was praying out loud and using most eloquent language. His prayer went something like this: 'O Thou who gildest the heavens and settest the stars in place, Thou who hast established the rocks and cliffs around our shores, against whose feet the heaving waters break in ineffectual foam. Thou whose might and power is known throughout the whole universe …'

After several minutes of this one man blurted out: 'That's enough. Ask Him for something. Ask, man, ask.' I wonder, are you someone who believes that grace drizzles over the whole of your life at a predetermined rate, no matter what you do? No extra effort on your part is required.

Asking makes it clear we are willing to receive.

Or perhaps you are one of those who believe that because God has been especially kind to you lately He should ignore you for a while and concentrate on someone else, someone more needy than you. This kind of thinking is a trap. Scripture repeatedly gives us examples of people who received things from God because they asked.

God instructs: 'Ask of me, and I will make the nations your inheritance.' Asking ensures that we do not take God for granted. As I said earlier, it tilts our soul in the direction of God. When we ask for grace it shows Him that we are in earnest about receiving it. Already we have made the point that when we ask for grace we do not need to wonder whether or not our prayer is in the will of God. God has made it clear He is willing to give; asking makes it clear we are willing to receive.

Further Study

Dan. 1:1–21; Neh. 1:1–2:9; 2 Cor. 4:1–18
1. What sustained both Nehemiah and Daniel?
2. What helped Paul not to lose heart?

Psa. 27:4–10; 119:1–16; Luke 11:1–13
3. What did the psalmist want more than anything else?
4. To those who seek, what did Jesus promise?

Psa. 5:1–12; 16:1–11; Acts 16:22–40
5. How did the psalmist express his dependence on God?
6. How did Paul and Silas express their dependence on God?

CHAPTER THREE

A VISION OF HOLINESS

2 Peter 3:1–18

Deuteronomy 4:15–31

Psalm 77:1–20

'Your ways, O God, are holy. What god
is so great as our God?'
Psalm 77:13

Another thing we must learn is this: although grace is free, it is not cheap. This is tremendously important because an overemphasis on grace to the exclusion of other important truths can lead to serious misunderstandings. As I have said before, truth not held in conjunction with other equally important truths can quickly become error.

A counsellor friend of mine recalls talking to a young married man who was involved in an extramarital affair. When he challenged the young man about this he responded: 'I know I'm wrong to continue my affair, but you're wrong to insist I end it. God doesn't want me to continue it I know, but He'll forgive me. I sense only judgement from you. God is a God of grace.' I can tell you this: Christians who hold the view that although God wants us to obey His commands it doesn't matter too much if we disregard them will never move forward in the Christian race. Deitrich Bonhoeffer, the German pastor who was executed by the Nazis just before the end of World War II, coined a phrase for this view of grace – he called it 'cheap grace'. He described it as 'cheap' because 'it does not consider what it cost God to make it available to us'. And what did it cost? It cost the humiliation, death, and resurrection of His only Son, the Lord Jesus Christ.

The more clearly we understand God's holiness and righteousness, and the more we consider how insistent He is in His Word that His children live as holy and righteous people, the more amazing is the concept of grace. 'The idea of "cheap grace",' says Dr Larry Crabb, 'develops when we talk about grace before we tremble at God's holiness.'

How do you see God?

Ask yourself this question right now: How do I see God? As an indulgent old grandfather who smiles at wrongdoing and says, 'He (or she) will get better as they get older,' or as a God who is awe-ful in His holiness?

C.S. Lewis, in his book *The Problem of Pain*, says that God is 'not ... a senile benevolence that drowsily wishes you to be happy in your own way ... but the consuming fire Himself'. The way we view God will be the way we approach Him. If we see Him as indulgent then we will approach Him with the kind of prayer I once came across in the Sunday bulletin of a liberal American church: 'We have done the best under difficult circumstances ... we have been badly influenced by our homes and environment ... so deal lightly with our lapses, be Your own sweet self with regard to our imperfections, and grant us the power to live harmless lives full of self-respect. Amen.'

Can it be, as Larry Crabb suggests, that our Christian culture has weakened our understanding of the holiness of God by introducing too soon the idea of grace? When I first considered that comment I winced. It seemed a devastating indictment, too painful to consider. But the more I thought about it the more I came to see that it is true. If we talk about grace in a way that makes God an indulgent figure who cares little or nothing about us measuring up to His standards then we have missed our way.

God's hatred of sin

The fact with which we must come to grips (especially those reading these lines who are preachers of the gospel) is that we are in serious trouble spiritually if we speak of grace in a way that changes the view of God from One who is the holy and righteous Judge to, in C.S. Lewis's phrase, 'a senile benevolence' – someone who wants us to come up to His standards but is indulgent when we don't.

If my experience is anything to go by, very few Christians today believe God hates sin. The picture many believers have of God nowadays is of someone who is so kind and considerate that He overlooks our moral lapses and encourages us to try harder next time so as not to fail. Personally, I blame many of today's preachers and evangelists for this state of affairs. Instead of starting (as does Billy Graham) with the bad news – that 'all have sinned and fall short of the glory of God' (Rom. 3:23) – they start with the good news – that God forgives all sin and is willing to receive us into heaven providing we submit to Jesus, His Son. But the presentation of the good news must be preceded by the bad news. This was how John Wesley preached. 'First,' he said, 'I present the law, then I sprinkle it with grace.'

Notice how Paul writes to the Romans: he presents God not as a loving Father who indulges all the people in His universe and wants them to have a good time. The Almighty, he says, is furious at everything that is sinful. The gospel begins with bad news before it goes on to give us the good news.

Our greatest need

I am asking you to reflect with me on the holiness, righteousness, and moral perfection of God. It is my conviction that the Church needs nothing greater at this time than a fresh vision of God's holiness. This is what every revival restores to the people of God – it gives them a sense that the God they are dealing with is a holy God. God's standards are perfect. Sometimes in the New Testament the term 'glory' is used to convey God's ideal. In Romans 3 verse 23 the word 'glory' is really shorthand for 'righteousness, perfection, and holiness'. Unlike us, God operates from a realm where all is absolute perfection. And here's some news that at first sounds bad for the men and women of this world: He requires the same of us. Everyone who hopes to relate to God must be righteous because He is righteous.

How different God is from His creation. To relate to

me, for example, you don't have to be perfect. If you told me your imperfections I would probably respond: 'I am not perfect myself, so I understand.' But God is not like that. He doesn't shrug His shoulders and say: 'That's OK.' There may be times when our goodness is highly commendable. We can take great moral strides and do some good deeds. But are we perfect? Never. By God's standards all human beings fall short.

The law of God was given to make clear to us how deserving of condemnation we are. J.B. Phillips translates Romans 3:20 in this way: 'Indeed it is the straight-edge of the Law that shows us how crooked we are.' How true. God is perfect, pure, spotless, and the laws He has made show us how imperfect, impure, and full of sin we are. We are pretty undeserving people. Were it not for grace where would we be?

A God most holy

A recovery of the sense of God's holiness is, I believe, essential for the contemporary Christian Church. If we do not see God as He is then we will never see ourselves as we are. One of the arguments put forward against Christianity is that by talking about a God who expects His children to live up to His standards we preachers have imposed upon people a sense of guilt and shame, which is an evil and mischievous thing. 'The things we do which the Church calls "sin",' says one writer, 'are very natural and we need not be ashamed of them. We should try not to do them, and if we hurt someone else then we must do our best to put things right, but there should never be any sense of shame.'

Our Lord Jesus Christ, when He came to this world, made it clear that He viewed men and women as essentially bad; that is why He preached repentance and the kingdom of God. Until we see that as true – that we are sinners in need of repentance – then we are not part of the audience to whom His words were addressed. Some people may think they are not the ones to whom He was referring but most assuredly they are. It is impossible to be a Christian without the preliminary consciousness of sin because without that there can be no real awareness of what it meant for a holy God to save us. The prayer of the hymnist needs to be ours also:

> *O make me understand it,*
> *Help me to take it in,*
> *What it meant for Thee,*
> *The Holy One,*
> *To take away my sin.*

Further Study

Psa. 24:1–10; 29:1–11; 1 Thess. 4:1–8; 1 Pet. 1:13–2:3
1. Who does the psalmist say will receive blessing from the Lord?
2. How does Peter exhort his readers?

Psa. 76:1–12; Amos 5:14–27; John 3:19–21; 3:27–36
3. What, according to Amos, are God's feelings about evil?

4. What is John the Baptist's testimony?

Psa. 86:1–17; Mark 10:32–45; Heb. 9:1–15
5. Affirm the character of God, along with the psalmist.
6. What does the death of Christ achieve, according to Hebrews?

LET GOD BE GOD

Titus 2:1–15

1 Peter 3:8–22

Romans 12:1–8

'*Therefore, I urge you, brothers, in view of God's mercy,
to offer your bodies as living sacrifices …*'
Romans 12:1

Whereof we understand what it cost God to offer His grace we will not abuse it. One question that is almost always raised when the subject of grace is discussed is this: If God is so full of grace doesn't this lead to an abuse of it on the part of His people? Won't they say: 'Because God is gracious and willing to forgive our sin we need not worry too much about sinning'? I have to admit that presenting the truth of grace to people is risky because there are those who would take it to the extreme.

This is the issue with which Paul is dealing in Romans 6. J.B. Phillips translates verses 1 and 2: 'Shall we sin to our heart's content and see how far we can exploit the grace of God? What a ghastly thought!' A ghastly thought indeed. Max Lucado puts it like this: 'Grace promoting evil? Mercy endorsing sin? What a horrible idea.' For those of you who are interested in Greek, the apostle here uses the strongest language possible to repudiate the idea: *Me genoito*, which means literally 'May it never be.' Anyone who regards grace as a licence to sin has failed to understand what grace is. 'Mercy understood,' said one writer, 'is holiness desired.' Those who have fathomed what it means to be forgiven by a holy God are so overwhelmed by His amazing grace that they want to give themselves to Him in holy living.

There are some who take advantage of grace, but you can be sure those who abuse it have never trembled at God's holiness and have little comprehension of what it means to be saved by grace. Indeed, I wonder if they have tasted God's mercy at all.

'A heart set to do good'

There is a phrase in the book of Titus that touches me deeply every time I read it. It is this: 'eager to do what is good' (2:14). Because we are the recipients of God's grace, His Holy Spirit fosters within us an eagerness to do good. We don't have to manufacture a desire to do good – the eagerness is already there because of grace. J.B. Phillips puts it like this: 'For he gave himself to us, that he might ... make for himself a people of his own, clean and pure, with our hearts set upon living a life that is good.' Grace does not spawn a desire to sin, it nurtures a desire to do good. You can be sure of this: the person who is truly aware of grace is a person who will not mock it. As I have said, the person who uses God's mercy and grace as a licence to sin shows that he or she has not understood grace at all. Personally, I doubt if such individuals are even saved.

> Grace nurtures a desire to do good.

But what if we do sin? What if we are overtaken by it and lapse by doing something that we know God abhors? Then, as John tells us: 'If anybody does sin, we have one who speaks to the Father in our defence – Jesus Christ, the Righteous One' (1 John 2:2). A true Christian will sometimes fall into sin, but he or she will not wallow in it. They will want to get right with God as quickly as they can and have the relationship restored. If they don't then you can be sure there is something seriously wrong with their conscience.

A professing Christian, a family member, once said to me: 'I am about to commit a serious sin, but I know that after I have done so God will be gracious to me and I will be restored.' I responded: 'But will you want to be restored?' He went on to commit the sin and now, over twenty years later, I have yet to see evidence of repentance.

The scent of danger

Everyone who gives teaching on grace must be aware that the truth can be pushed to extremes. In W.H. Auden's poem 'For the Time Being' the attitude of those who abuse grace is summed up in the following words: 'Every crook will argue: "I like committing crimes. God likes forgiving them. Really the world is admirably arranged."'

The fear that people will take grace to an extreme prevents many ministers from emphasising it. A preacher friend of mine commented: 'If I emphasise grace in the way you are telling me I should then run the risk that people will misunderstand it and be less responsible about the way they live.' Dr Martyn Lloyd-Jones, the great Bible expositor, once declared: 'I would say to all you preachers: if your preaching of the message that salvation is all of grace has not been understood then you had better examine your sermons once again, and you had better make sure you really are preaching the salvation that is offered in the New Testament to the ungodly, to the sinner, to those who are enemies of God. There is this kind of dangerous element about the true presentation of the doctrine of salvation.' Grace has about it the scent of danger. Yes, it can be misused, but it is only misused when it is misunderstood.

When people say to me, 'My problem is that I can't forgive,' I usually respond: 'No, that is not your problem. Your problem is you don't know how much you have been forgiven.' Why do I say that? Because the power for Christian living comes from focusing on what God has done for us in Christ. Though I have said this before it must be repeated: grace may have come to us freely but it was obtained at the greatest cost.

'The scandal of grace'

The point cannot be overemphasised: a person who sees grace as permission to sin has missed the meaning of grace entirely. The quotation I included earlier is important enough to repeat: 'Mercy understood is holiness desired.' When I asked one of God's 'pacesetters' many years ago how he was able to balance God's desire for us to live holy lives with the fact that grace is available to cover every sin he replied: 'I treat grace as an undeserved privilege, not as an exclusive right.' This will help you, too, to keep your balance. Live gratefully, not arrogantly.

One writer, a secularist, wrote about what he called 'the scandal of grace'. This is what he said: 'God wants people to live righteous lives but then He does the strange thing of offering forgiveness in advance. He also says that the more sin increases the more grace increases. It's a scandalous doctrine and doesn't make any sense. Why be good if you know in advance you are going to be forgiven? Why not be like the pagans – eat, drink, and be merry for tomorrow we die?'

Well, grace may seem scandalous to the uninitiated, but to those of us who have tasted of it, it is the most wonderful gift in the universe. Let me spell it out once again: holiness demands that sin needs to be punished. Grace compels that the sinner be loved. How can God do both? 1 Peter 3 verse 18 gives the answer. The perfect record that belongs to Christ has been given to us, and our imperfect record has been given to Him. He suffered, the righteous for the unrighteous, to bring us to God. When first heard and understood this seems too good to be true. But in reality it is too good not to be true!

Live gratefully, not arrogantly.

Mercy – the motive

Paul's provocative question 'Shall we go on sinning, so that grace may increase?' (Rom. 6:1) has provided a talking-point throughout the ages. Philip Yancey has an excellent response to that question. He pictures a young man saying to his bride: 'I love you very much, but I am sure you will not mind me having a few affairs now and then. You are a forgiving person so just think of the opportunities for enjoyment you will get in forgiving me.'

To such a remark, says Yancey, the only reasonable reaction from the bride would be a slap in the face and a 'God forbid!' By his attitude the bridegroom would be demonstrating that he did not understand the first thing about love. Similarly, if our attitude as far as God is concerned is to see how much we can get away with then it proves we do not have any idea what He has in mind for us. Indeed, it is questionable if someone with that frame of mind understands the meaning of salvation at all.

In Romans 12 verse 1 Paul urges the believers in Rome to offer their bodies as living sacrifices 'in view of God's mercy'. In other words, the incentive for doing good is gratitude for what has been done for us. Those who try to live the Christian life out of a sense of duty are living under law, not grace. This is why Paul begins all of his letters with a reminder of what Christ has done for us and the riches we have through grace. We should strive for holiness not in order to make God love us but because He already does.

When we truly grasp the wonder of God's grace the question raised by devious individuals that Paul repeated would never occur to us. As Yancey says: 'We would spend all our days trying to fathom, not exploit, God's grace.'

'God – the infinite Reality'

It is one thing to ask God for grace but it is another to open our heart to receive it. As someone has commented: 'It's no good God pouring His grace in abundant measure into our lives if the flow is blocked by an inability to receive.' We have to know how to let grace into our lives, how to take down the barriers, how to become open to it. In fact, we must permit it to permeate us so completely that it floods our souls.

On my computer I have a file headed 'Quotable Quotes'. While looking for a quote on the subject we are thinking about now – receiving grace – I came across this by E.S. Jones: 'God, the infinite Reality, is pervading us and invading us, and the pathway over which He comes to the centre of our being is the pathway of receptivity.' I would have been tempted to say 'relaxed receptivity', but perhaps for receptivity to be receptivity it must be relaxed. 'You cannot inscribe anything on a tense anxious mind,' said the same writer, 'for receptivity is the surrendering of all fears, all doubts, all inhibitions, especially the self, for the ego, even in God's presence, asserts itself, wants to be God. It must be surrendered.'

Whenever I have spoken or written on the subject of surrender I have found that people's usual response is to say: 'It's easy to talk about surrender but how do you do it?' Let us therefore spend some time thinking through this issue because you can be sure of this: 'pacesetters' are people who have surrendered their ego to the Lord and know how to let God be God.

Taking second place

If the expression – 'let God be God' – is new to you then

let me explain it to you. Our ego was never meant to be central to our personality – despite what modern psychologists say. We were made to have God at the centre of our beings and for the ego to revolve around Him. Thus we are designed not to be ego-centred but God-centred. To let God be God is to surrender our ego into His hands. When we do that then we function as we were designed to.

I must emphasise that surrender does not mean collapse. Some, I am afraid, see it in that way; they believe surrender involves becoming ciphers and living before God with what someone has described as mushy meaninglessness. Surrender, when properly understood, means that we have a better chance of fulfilling our potential because we are living according to God's design. A truly surrendered person offers to God an alert self, no longer eager for its own way but for the way – a self knowing its place is second, and eager to serve the First. Once, when talking to a Christian lady about surrender, she asked me: 'If I surrender everything to the Lord does that mean I become pulp?' 'Of course not,' I replied. 'In fact, you become more of a person; you become a person with a controlling purpose – the purpose of following the Person who is above all persons.'

Everybody surrenders to something. One writer puts it like this: 'Everyone goes into the shrine of the heart and bends the knee to something, something that has the place of supreme allegiance.' Can I ask what you bow the knee to?

The last thing we give up

Some bow the knee to what others think of them. They don't act, they react. Others bend the knee to themselves. Self-interest is supreme. There are many other things – money, sex, ambition – which may be the centre of devotion. Each one of us must whisper the consent of abdication before grace can flow into our souls in all its fullness. You must say to yourself: 'I am not the one who is supreme. God is. I bow the knee to Him and to Him alone.'

But didn't we do that at conversion? Yes, we did in a measure. But rarely is it done wholly. As we grow in Christ we see other areas that must be surrendered. The conscious mind is given to Him at conversion but now the subconscious mind – the cause of our divisions and clashes – must be laid at His feet as well. Jesus says with awful decisiveness: 'If anyone comes to me and does not hate his father and mother ...' Then He makes this statement: 'yes, even his own life – he cannot be my disciple.' Why did He put 'life' last? Because it's the last thing we surrender.

A missionary once told me: 'I gave up my home, family, friends, church, to come to a foreign land. I gave up everything except myself.' To go into the ministry I gave up a career in engineering, but then I found myself preaching the gospel with a great deal of vanity and personal ambition. It is possible to give up lots of things without giving up the self. You see, that is where our life is – in the self. It must be surrendered.

Further Study

Psa. 37:1–40; Eph. 4:17–32; Heb. 13:15–21

1. Along with the psalmist, contrast the wicked with those who do good.
2. How does Paul encourage the Ephesians to live godly lives?

Deut. 10:12–11:32; Mark 1:14–20; Col. 1:15–23

3. How important was it for Israel to remain God-centred?
4. How important was it to Paul to be Christ-centred?

Psa. 14:1–7; Luke 12:13–34; John 12:20–26; Col. 3:1–17

5. What is God looking for, according to the psalmist?
6. On what should we set our hearts, according to Paul?

CHAPTER FIVE

LIVING FOR HIM

2 Corinthians 5:11–21

1 Peter 5:1–7

Hebrews 12:1–17

*'And he died for all, that those who live should no longer
live for themselves but for him who died for them …'*
2 Corinthians 5:15

Perhaps you are still finding it difficult to make a full surrender to God. Frequently I have spent time with people who were struggling to surrender completely to the Lord and, as I have watched them, it has seemed as if they were about to say a final farewell to a loved one – the loved one in this case being the self. As I encouraged one young woman to pray a prayer of full surrender she blurted out: 'But if I surrender everything to God then I will be at His mercy.' She thought God was looking for a chance to make her miserable because she did not understand that His will and her best interests were one and the same.

In the first decade of my Christian life I struggled very much with this idea of surrender, as I have often mentioned in the past. For a long while I believed that if I surrendered fully to God He would make me marry a girl whom I found unattractive and send me as a missionary to some remote part of the world. In fact, I had been in the ministry for a few years before I finally said 'Yes' to God on everything. From that moment I have not belonged to myself. I let go of the one thing I owned – myself.

One 'pacesetter' I know explains how he maintains a continuous attitude of surrender. 'I begin every day by spending some time sitting in God's presence. After studying His Word, I invite Him to show me if there are any barriers preventing His grace coming through. Mostly nothing is shown me, and by faith I take it that the doors of my soul are open to Him. Sometimes He does show me a hindrance, fear, or jealousy. I repent and ask His forgiveness, resolve to put things right, and, after a time of intercession, I go out into the day, serene and secure.'

Paul – a magnificent model

No one has been a more surrendered person than the apostle Paul. What a magnificent model he is for us in this matter of receiving grace. One of the reasons why he was so open to God's grace was because, as he tells us in Philippians 3, he put no confidence in the flesh. What was his flesh like? What was it like to be in Paul's skin before he became a Christian? Read once again and try to imagine.

He was 'circumcised on the eighth day, of the people of Israel, of the tribe of Benjamin, a Hebrew of Hebrews; in regard to the law, a Pharisee; as for zeal, persecuting the church; as for legalistic righteousness, faultless' (vv.5–6). 'That's my record,' Paul is saying. 'It may look impressive in the sight of the world but in the eyes of God I was lost and in great need.'

He got his priorities straight.

Notice how he states that fact: 'But whatever was to my profit I now consider loss for the sake of Christ' (v.7). A few lines further on he says: 'What is more, I consider everything a loss compared to the surpassing greatness of knowing Christ Jesus my Lord, for whose sake I have lost all things. I consider them rubbish, that I may gain

Christ and be found in him' (vv.8–9). Paul had a great track record but he did not rely on it. He got his priorities straight. When that happened everything fell into place. Once he had no confidence in the flesh he became more open to receiving God's grace.

Those who master the inner struggle and put no confidence in the flesh become wonderful recipients of God's grace. They move along the path of Christian discipleship at a rapid rate. Do you know what life is like for people like that? Fantastic! Though problems still arise they are able to handle them with God's help.

Go away and be humble

We have talked a good deal about the need for surrender, but there is one thing more I would like to say about becoming good receivers of God's grace: an attitude of humility is essential.

When I talk about humility the statement made by the preacher Phillips Brooks always springs into my mind: 'The true way to be humble is not to stoop until you are smaller than yourself but to stand at your real height against some higher nature that will show you what the real smallness of your greatest greatness is.' So stand at your real height, look up at God, reflect on His greatness, holiness, and majesty, and consider how infinitely bigger than you He is. Then go away and be for ever humble. When you lose sight of God then the self begins to loom large. A man once told me: 'I used to believe in God but now I don't believe in Him at all. I am coming round to believe that I myself am all-important.' When we lose God we lose our source of humility.

After writing that last sentence my telephone rang, and during the conversation that followed a friend asked me which theme I was writing on. When I told him I was exploring the subject of humility, he said: 'In the Christian Church I think only the humble can lead, for people who parade their virtues are not fit to lead a procession. We cannot inwardly respond to the proud, however spiritual they may appear to be. Put that into your book.' So I have, not just because he asked me to but because what he said fits perfectly with what we have been saying.

Graduating in grace

To move on and mature in the Christian faith we must realise that grace has to be used before more is given. In John 1:16, a text we looked at earlier – 'from the fulness of his grace we have all received one blessing after another' – the phrase one blessing after another can be translated in several different ways. The New King James Version uses the words 'grace for grace'. J.B. Phillips' translation says: 'there is a grace in our lives because of his grace'. A number of translations use the phrase 'grace upon grace'. When I looked at this verse in a Welsh version I found a word that in English would be best translated as 'succeeding': 'grace succeeding grace'. This, I believe, perfectly captures John's meaning. We must use the grace God gives us in the present to be ready to use the grace which will then succeed it.

One preacher I know claims that we graduate in the use of grace. 'A man can't walk into a university,' he says, 'and submit himself for a doctorate. He must be a Master first in his field of study. He can't walk in and submit himself for a Master; he must be a Bachelor first. It is only as you absorb learning at one level that you are able to absorb it at a higher level. So it is with grace. We advance. We graduate.' The point he is making is that if we do not avail ourselves of God's grace at one stage then we will not be offered further supplies at a later stage.

> Grace has to be used before more is given.

There is an old saying about there being no short cuts on a straight road. The Christian life is a straight road and we proceed along it one step at a time. We can't miss out any of the intermediate steps. Present grace must be used before future grace is given.

Step by step

Many have slowed down on the path of Christian discipleship because, by refusing God's grace at one stage, they prevented themselves from receiving it at a later stage.

Over the years I have talked to many believers who told me that they began the Christian life with zest and vigour and moved with speed along the path of Christian discipleship. Then they slackened off, and it became questionable whether they were moving at all. When I have been involved in counselling such people I have found that there was a time in their lives when God had led them to some new level of surrender, but for some reason they had pulled back. Perhaps it was a new task He wanted them to take up, a challenge about their management of time, a direct appeal to use the talents they had been given, or a word about the need to deal more carefully with their finances. But they had ignored His voice and followed their own inclinations.

I cannot emphasise this fact too strongly: whenever there has been a slowing down and a slackening off in spiritual things it can always be traced back to some sin of commission or omission. You see, whenever God gives us a task or a challenge He also provides the grace which enables us to rise to it. By refusing the task or the challenge we refuse the grace. And that's when we run on to the sandbank. Refusal to receive the grace at that point means we are not offered subsequent supplies of grace. Grace is there, rolling in like the waves of the sea, but we must use the grace first given to be able to use the grace that succeeds it.

> But they had ignored His voice.

Corresponding grace
Some Christians I know claim their slowing down on the path of Christian discipleship was due to the fact that God (so they believe) did not provide the grace they

needed at a given time. Here is one example.

A man once told me this: 'It is impossible for me to be a Christian in the place where I work. I find myself falling in with the others – using the occasional swear word, telling a smutty story now and again. I try hard to be different, but I end up being one of the lads. What is said about God giving grace in every situation doesn't seem to be true in my case.' As we talked together and discussed his past I discovered that although he attended church regularly and was involved in some of its ministries he was addicted to pornography and had in his pocket at the time he was speaking to me a set of what we call 'dirty postcards'. 'How did this addiction begin?' I asked. 'It began,' he said, 'when my girlfriend, who was also a Christian, broke up with me. A few hours later I found myself outside an Adult Book Store and before I knew it I was inside. For two hours, as I looked at the magazines and videos, all my pain went away. From then on I have found pornography to be a great pain reliever.'

I pointed out to this man that the very moment he was standing at the entrance to the Adult Book Store the grace of God was flowing towards him like a tidal river. The problem was not that God's grace was unavailable; the problem was he did not respond to it. Refusing grace at that point, and failing to repent of his lapse into pornography, made him unable to employ it subsequently. When we lapse spiritually it is wrong to blame God. With every divine command comes corresponding grace.

Missed grace

What an interesting instruction we find in Hebrews 12: see to it that no one misses the grace of God. How can God's grace be missed? Well, think back to the man I mentioned earlier, the one who went into the Adult Book Store. You can be sure that the moment he was being tempted to go into that place the grace of God was flowing towards him. He had a choice – to either avail himself of it or to refuse it. Instead of turning to the grace which God offered he turned to the temptation and ended up soiling his soul. That's what it means to miss the grace of God.

Hebrews 12:15–17 says that three main problems arise when we miss God's grace. Before considering them let me say that the best translation of this passage, in my opinion, is that provided for us by J.B. Phillips: 'Be careful that none of you fails to respond to the grace which God gives, for if he does there can very easily spring up in him a bitter spirit which is not only bad in itself but can also poison the lives of many others' (v.15).

Imagine hearing that a friend has been saying some bad things about you. Now remember, at the very moment the matter is made known to you the grace of God is flowing towards you to enable you to deal with it in a spiritual way. But you refuse the grace, and now what happens? Your spirit becomes bitter, and because bitterness is not a pleasant feeling you spread it around a little. You fly off the handle at the slightest thing, and your friends and family feel the effect of your bitterness.

'What's wrong with him (or her)?' they say. You know what's wrong. Grace was there to help you deal with the issue in a Christlike way but you missed it.

No grace – no strength

One possible result of missing or refusing the grace of God is the development of a bitter spirit. Another one is the possibility of falling into impurity. We need grace to live pure lives, and when that grace is missed or refused we become extremely vulnerable to temptation, especially impure thoughts or deeds.

This is what happened to the man to whom I referred earlier. He found sexual titillation to be an effective painkiller and his mind became, in words used by Dr W.E. Sangster, a 'merry-go-round of lustful images and impure thoughts'. Most of us feel powerful urges, especially in the realm of sex. However, God has provided us, through His grace, with the strength to control these urges, and build a life in which morals regulate the appetites. If we miss the grace we will also miss the moral strengthening that comes with it.

> We need grace to live pure lives.

The third possible consequence of missing or refusing the grace which God gives is that we can lose our reverence for the things of God. Esau did this, says the writer to the Hebrews; he was more concerned with the present than the future. One of the effects of God's grace is that it enables us to measure the things of time against the things of eternity. Self-gratification becomes secondary and is superseded by a desire to discover the purposes of God and bring Him glory. Esau failed by valuing food for his stomach more highly than his birthright (see Gen. 25:29–34). So let this solemn word sink deep into your heart: 'Be careful that none of you fails to respond to the grace of God, for if he does ...' (v.15, Phillips).

Further Study
Psa. 51:1–17; Acts 3:11–26
1. What is the psalmist's chief desire?
2. What is the main focus of Peter's exhortation?

Num. 12:1–15; Prov. 3:34; Matt. 11:25–30; Luke 14:1–11
3. What sort of person was Moses?
4. What characteristic did Jesus both display and commend?

2 Sam. 11:1–27; 1 Cor. 10:1–13
5. What resulted from David's disobedience?
6. What warning and what promise does Paul give?

CHAPTER SIX

'THE AROMA OF GRACE'

Revelation 2:1–7

Philippians 2:1–11

Romans 15:1–13

*'Accept one another, then, just as Christ accepted you,
in order to bring praise to God.'*
Romans 15:7

We have learnt so far that we must use the grace offered to us in the present in order to use the grace that succeeds it. The Christian life is a step-by-step progression, and we cannot cut out any step. If we think God overlooks our violations of His standards and says, 'You missed a step back there but it's all right, carry on and make sure you don't miss one again,' then we are greatly mistaken. Can I prove this point biblically? Most certainly.

Take the case of the Ephesian church. In one sense the Ephesian Christians were wonderful people, and were commended by the Lord for their good deeds, hard work and perseverance (Rev. 2:2). Yet they had missed a step in their Christian walk – they had forsaken their first love. How does the Saviour deal with this problem? Does He say: 'I have drawn your attention to this so that you don't fall into this situation again. Now regain your first love and I will say no more about it'? Christ is too good a counsellor to deal with the issue in that way. In verse 5 He points out three things they need to do.

One is to remember the height from which they had fallen. 'Think about the way things were,' He is telling them, 'the heights to which you had risen in the things of God.' Remembering this would help their spiritual perspective. His second command is repent. This is the only way to deal with a missed step. There must be genuine repentance, a turning back to God in humble recognition that one has missed the way. It is not a matter of kissing and making up. There must be heartfelt

contrition. Then return: 'do the things you did at first.'
Notice that returning is the last step, not the first.

Making our 'me' gracious

'Pacesetters' know not only how to receive grace but also
how to pass it on to others.

There is a charming, though probably apocryphal,
story which has come down to us relating to the
childhood of England's present queen, Elizabeth II. It
tells how, as a small girl, she was puzzled about the words
her father, King George VI, used during the singing of

Grace is meant to be
demonstrated.

the national anthem since it
began 'God save our
gracious King.' As he
himself was the king, she
wondered if he sang to

himself 'God save the gracious me.' One thing is certain:
if we do not allow God to make our 'me' gracious then
the purpose of His grace is thwarted. He pours His grace
into us that we might pour it out to others.

It is here that many of us, myself included, have to put
up our hands and confess that while we may be good
receivers of grace, we are not always good dispensers of
it. During a discussion programme on TV in which a
group of people were talking about the amazing grace of
God one sceptic asked: 'If grace is so amazing why don't
Christians show more of it?' There is enough truth
behind that question to sting. Charles Swindoll says:
'Grace is not something simply to be claimed; it is meant

to be demonstrated. It is to be shared, used as a basis for friendships and drawn upon for sustained relationships.'

So often grace is stifled in relationships. We can be going along fine until someone upsets us, and then showing grace to that person is something we fail to do. We may prefer to avoid these issues, but not to confront them is to miss one of God's steps.

Not sufficiently Christlike

'If grace is so amazing why don't Christians show more of it?' That is the issue with which we must come to grips with. Many of us feel we have 'arrived' when, by faith, we are accepted into the family of God. But a Christian, far from having arrived, is always on the road as a follower of Christ.

There is a prayer, I understand, that has become legendary in Washington. It was offered at an informal White House prayer group by a Jewish man named Arthur Burns, at that time chairman of the United States Federal Reserve System and a man of some distinction. Though not a Christian he seemed to find pleasure in being present at the prayer meetings. Naturally the Christians there treated him with respect even though they found it difficult to involve him in the proceedings. For example, different people would be asked to close in prayer but Arthur Burns would always be passed by. However, one day the group was led by a newcomer who did not know the situation. At the end of the session he turned to Arthur Burns and asked him to close in prayer.

For a moment he hesitated, and then he prayed this prayer: 'Lord, I pray that You would bring Jews to know Jesus Christ. I pray that You would bring Muslims to know Jesus Christ. Finally, Lord, I pray that You would bring Christians to know Jesus Christ. Amen.'

His refreshing directness quite startled those present, but they took the point: those who already know Jesus Christ need to know Him better if they are to reflect His amazing grace to the world around. Rarely are Christians indicted for being too much like their Lord; far more commonly they are charged with not being sufficiently Christlike.

The blight of disunity

We must face the fact that we Christians, generally speaking, do not reflect or relay to others the grace we have been given in the way we ought. Critics of Christianity rarely criticise Christ; their criticisms are reserved for the followers of Christ who so poorly represent Him. Friedrich Nietzsche said: 'In truth there was only one Christian and He died on a cross.' George Bernard Shaw quipped: 'Christianity might be a good thing if anyone tried it.'

Take the matter of unity, for example, for which Christ prayed in John 17. Clearly unity is important to Jesus Christ. Francis Schaeffer said that God has given the world the right to judge whether or not Christianity is true by the way Christians live in unity with one another. Our heavenly Father does not want His children to squabble. Disunity disturbs Him greatly. And why? Because 'By this all men will know that you are my disciples, if you love one another' (John 13:35). Do you realise what Jesus meant when He said those words? Read this next sentence carefully: the unity of believers will encourage men and women to believe that Jesus is who He said He was. That means not just agreeing with one another, or solving all our differences, but loving one another, showing grace to one another. Disunity fosters unbelief. 'Who wants to get on board a ship of bickering sailors?' asks Max Lucado. And Paul Billhemir writes: 'The sin of disunity has caused more souls to be lost than all other sins combined.'

Throughout time writers and preachers have called the Church to unity, but we still have a long way to go. Could it be that disunity is the reason why we are not winning the world to Christ?

The choice is yours

We linger on the subject of disunity among the people of God – a matter that is of great importance to our heavenly Father and, consequently, should be to us also. The cause of disunity is clear: it comes about because we fail to dispense to others the grace we ourselves have received from God. Ephesians 4 verse 3 urges us to 'keep the unity of the Spirit through the bond of peace'. There is an unbreakable unity in the Trinity which God desires to see reflected in the Church.

Think of this: there has never been an argument

among the members of the Trinity, never a quarrel, never a disagreement. Why, sometimes we find it difficult to get on with one another for a few days; the Father, Son, and Holy Spirit have existed for all eternity without a single dispute. Unity matters to each member of the Trinity, and matters to them more than we can ever realise. Then shouldn't unity matter to us? Notice that our text does not tell us to build unity; we are simply instructed to keep it. From God's point of view there is one flock and one Shepherd (see John 10:16). Unity is not something to be created but something to be protected.

Shouldn't unity matter to us?

But how do we do that? How do we 'make every effort to keep the unity of the Spirit'? Do we abandon our convictions, compromise our beliefs, water down our doctrines? No, but when a dispute does arise we must make the effort to disagree agreeably. God has created us as choosing beings. We can choose to be either gracious or ungracious. The next time you feel you have to disagree with someone remember you have a choice: you can disagree disagreeably or disagree agreeably. The choice is always yours.

'The fumes of ungrace'
'How is it,' says one writer, 'that Christians called to dispense the aroma of grace instead emit the noxious fumes of ungrace?' How indeed? Permit this personal

question: If you have a problem in dispensing 'the aroma of grace' in your relationships are you willing to make every effort to discover why? Assuming your answer is 'Yes', let me see if I can help you.

One of the first things to consider is the need to accept people as they are. This has been described as 'the first law in good relationships'. Keep in mind that acceptance does not mean approval; it means accepting that the person is the way he or she is and that you respect them as persons even though you cannot approve of anything that is unbiblical.

From Mark 9 we discover that the disciples had been arguing with each other about which of them was the greatest. Jesus responded by standing a child in their midst and saying: 'Whoever welcomes [or accepts] one of these little children in my name welcomes me' (v.37). The point Jesus was making was this: acceptance is the first step to unity. Not agreement, not approval, not negotiation, not arbitration – acceptance. John was troubled by this answer and thought it too simplistic. Perhaps he said in effect: 'We saw someone casting out demons in Your Name. Do we accept him? Surely we can't always go around accepting everyone.' Clearly, the Son of Thunder (see Mark 3:17) had a problem with acceptance. His view was that fences have to be built, agreements negotiated, boundaries established – all very necessary perhaps in some situations. But not in this case. How accepting are little children. We must make the effort to be the same.

A long way to go

We have said that 'the first law of relationships' is acceptance. This is a skill that with thought and consideration anyone can put into effect, but it is a skill made easier by grace. There are many other things we may need to know about dispensing grace, but it is outside the scope of this book to go into them one by one. I am focusing only on acceptance because that is the first step to unity. Unless we learn this then all the other skills, such as negotiating, establishing boundaries, and so on, will not come together.

Paul, in chapter 14 of his letter to the Romans, had raised the matter of whether or not it was right to eat meat – obviously something the believers were struggling with. How does he advise them to deal with their disagreement? By having two churches – one for the meat eaters and one for vegetarians? No, he says: 'Accept one another, then, just as Christ accepted you (Rom. 15:7).' In asking us, through Paul, to accept each other, God is not telling us to do something He has not done. If God can tolerate my mistakes (though, of course, He cannot tolerate sin) then ought I not to tolerate yours? If God allows me, a man with a history of mistakes and failures, to call Him Father shouldn't I extend the same grace to you? Shame on me if I don't.

The Church, someone has commented, is like Noah's ark. If it wasn't for the storm on the outside we wouldn't be able to stand the stench on the inside. We have a long way to go to demonstrate the degree of unity which the

Father has with the Son – the unity for which Christ prayed in John 17. Do you think our Lord would pray a prayer that had no possibility of being answered? I don't think so either.

'Brother- and sister-bashers'

How different the Church would appear in the eyes of the world if all Christians related to each other with grace. One preacher I know refers to Christians who can't get along with each other as 'brother- and sister-bashers'. And there are already too many of them roaming around on the spiritual scene. Nothing catches the attention of the world more than Christians coming to blows with each other. Paul, in Ephesians 6:10 (NKJV), talks about wrestling not with flesh and blood but with principalities and powers. How sad when we believers reverse that and spend our time wrestling not with principalities and powers but with flesh and blood.

A while ago I read about something humorous that happened in connection with two evangelistic crusades that were held in an American city, one immediately after the other. The venue for both crusades was a small indoor stadium in the city. In between the crusades, and for one night only, a wrestling match had been booked. Those entering the stadium for the first crusade were amused to see the announcement in lights over the stadium entrance:

Programme for the next two weeks:
Evangelist Jack Van Impe
Wrestling
Rex Humbard

If the world is to be won for Jesus Christ then we simply must take this matter of relating to one another in grace more seriously. We owe it to Christ, to each other, and to the world to do so.

Further Study

2 Sam. 9:1–13; Philem. 1–25; 1 John 2:7–14
1. How did David show God's kindness?
2. Why did Paul ask Philemon to forgive Onesimus?

Psa. 45:1–7; John 4:1–26; 1 John 3:10–20
3. In what ways did God's grace flow out of Jesus?
4. In what ways should God's grace flow out of us?

Rom. 14:1–23; 1 Thess. 5:8–15
5. What is Paul's advice on disputable matters?
6. How did Paul exhort the Thessalonians?

CHAPTER SEVEN

STILL FEELING INDEBTED?

Matthew 18:21–35

Luke 7:36–50

Romans 6:15–23

'The servant's master took pity on him, cancelled
the debt and let him go.'
Matthew 18:27

One more thing we must learn is how to enter into the freedom that grace provides and understand that the Master has forgiven us an insurmountable debt and that He doesn't demand reimbursement. 'Ah,' I hear you say, 'I believe that but I wouldn't think of myself as a "pacesetter".' Well, let's consider this matter carefully for you may find that though you believe it in your head it has not yet reached your heart. After years of listening to people talking about their problems I have come to the conclusion that by far the biggest single difficulty evangelical Christians struggle with is the failure to live a 'debt-free' existence. Let me explain.

The servant in the passage we have read today had a serious problem. Somehow he had run up a massive debt; the Amplified Bible tells us it was 'probably about 10 million dollars'. Now it is important to realise that Jesus is deliberately using an exaggerated amount here to make it clear that the servant's debt was far greater than his ability to pay. That's the main point Jesus is making here. The king to whom he owed the debt decided to call it in and ordered the servant to take immediate steps for its repayment. Falling to his knees, the servant begs for time to pay, whereupon the king decides to cancel the debt and set him free.

The servant then goes out and comes across a man who owes him a mere pittance (about 20 dollars, says the Amplified Bible) and, because he is unable to repay the money, has him put in prison. Why did he act in this way? There is only one explanation: he still felt in debt. The good news he had been given was still in his head and had never reached his heart.

No little sins

We continue reflecting on the story told in Matthew 18:21–35 of the servant who, having been forgiven a massive debt, goes out and demands that a man who owes him a paltry sum be cast into prison. Something is wrong with this picture. It doesn't make sense that a man forgiven such a large sum would behave in this way towards someone who owed him such an insignificant amount. The account says: 'He grabbed him and began to choke him. "Pay back what you owe me!" he demanded' (Matt. 18:28). Are these the words of a man who has been set free? How could this happen? How could a man who was forgiven not forgive?

How could a man who was forgiven not forgive?

We touched on the answer earlier: he did not feel forgiven. The servant left the king's presence a free man, but he had not allowed the impact of such amazing grace to penetrate his heart. His problem was unrealised forgiveness. Many Christians are in this same state. They have been forgiven a massive debt – far beyond their power to repay – but the realisation of just how much they have been forgiven has never quite hit them. Their debt to God has been discharged through the payment made by Christ on Calvary's cross, but they seem unable to enter into the freedom such a release should bring.

Are you in this state, I wonder? Has the realisation of how much you have been forgiven reached deep into your heart? Then take some time today to ponder just what it means to be forgiven. If you think you have committed only little sins then think again. There are no little sins because there is no little God to sin against. Your sins deserved eternal death, and were it not for the death of the Son of God that is what would have been in store for you.

From minimum to maximum

The issue of unrealised forgiveness is an important one so we will spend some more time reflecting on it. Jesus puts His finger on the matter we are discussing. Eugene Peterson, in *The Message* (Luke 7), expresses Jesus' words in this way: 'If the forgiveness is minimal, the gratitude is minimal.' 'Pacesetters', I have discovered, don't have a problem with unrealised forgiveness. They have a clear awareness that they have been forgiven a massive debt, a debt it would have been absolutely impossible for them to repay even if they had been given all eternity to repay it. And they are grateful for that forgiveness, more grateful than words can ever convey.

Focusing on the extent to which we have been forgiven is vital to the rest of our Christian life. Awareness of forgiveness brings not only feelings of freedom and gratitude to God but also a willingness to forgive those who have sinned against us. You see, only the truly forgiven can be forgiving. The truth is this: our pockets are empty while our debt runs into millions. We don't need a better salary in order to pay off the debt over a lifetime, we need a gift. Max Lucado says: 'We don't need swimming lessons, we need a lifesaver.'

Perhaps it was not possible for you to follow the suggestion I made earlier to find a quiet place and ponder just how much you have been forgiven. If that was the case then try to do so now. Realise the enormity of the debt you owed to God and the grace He showed you in cancelling it. Think about that until your heart awakens fully to the news that the massive debt you owed to God has been forgiven. Forgiven!

'Remember the duck'

One of the consequences of unrealised forgiveness and of not entering into the freedom which forgiveness is meant to bring is that we become extremely vulnerable to Satan's accusations. Countless times I have counselled Christians who, though they have been forgiven, are still troubled by feelings of guilt. And nothing pleases Satan more than to find Christians in that condition for he knows that his accusations will find their mark.

Recently I read about a young boy and his sister who spent their summer holiday on their grandmother's farm. One day, while the boy was throwing stones, he accidentally hit his grandmother's pet duck and killed it. Rather than owning up, he took the duck and hid it in thick undergrowth. His sister, however, had witnessed the incident, and for a few days afterwards, whenever she wanted to persuade her brother to do something, she would whisper: 'Remember the duck.' Eventually the boy grew tired of being manipulated and confessed to his grandmother what he had done. To his surprise she said: 'I was standing at the window and saw what you did myself. Because I love you I decided to forgive you. But I did wonder how long you would let your sister make a slave out of you.'

So many Christians are in a similar position; they have been pardoned but they are slaves to the accuser (the name given to Satan in Revelation 12:10). Satan has no higher goal than to take you to court and press charges. He paces backwards and forwards before God's bench calling your name, listing your faults, naming your sins. Listen: because Jesus shed His blood for you on Calvary the Judge has released you. You are free. You need no longer fear the court.

You are free.

The first principle
Nothing is more vital if we are to live effectively as Christians than entering into the freedom that grace provides. It is one thing to be pronounced free but it is another thing to feel free. The issue of unrealised forgiveness, I believe, is the chief cause of a failure to forgive others. If we really understood how much we

have been forgiven then we would have little difficulty in forgiving others. The sins others have committed against you (though they may be vile) cannot compare with the massive debt you built up by your denial of God's right to rule in your heart.

I realise that those of you reading these lines who have been the victim of such evils as sexual abuse or brutality may find that difficult to accept. I would not judge you or condemn you if you said: 'I can never forgive that person for what he (or she) did to me.' But what I would say to you is this: the more you reflect on the wonder of how much you have been forgiven the easier it will be to forgive even the worst sins that have been committed against you.

There are many principles to consider in relation to forgiveness, but this without any doubt is the first principle: the more we realise how much we have been forgiven the more forgiving we will be. I was interested to read this in Dr David Seamand's book *Healing Grace*: 'I am convinced that the basic cause of some of the most disturbing emotional and spiritual problems which trouble evangelical Christians is the failure to receive and live out God's unconditional grace and the corresponding failure to offer that grace to others. I encounter this problem in the counselling room more than any other hang-up.' And so, I must add, have I.

Further Study

Deut. 15:1–15; Gal 2:15–21
1. Why was cancelling debts important in Israel's life?
2. How did Paul describe his own life in Christ?

Dan. 9:1–19; Eph. 1:1–10
3. What is the main import of Daniel's prayer?
4. What are the chief blessings for those in Christ?

Psa. 112:1–9; 2 Cor. 8:1–15; Phil. 4:10–20
5. What comes to the man who fears the Lord?
6. For what does Paul give thanks?

CHAPTER EIGHT

A CHILD OF HIS GRACE

2 Timothy 1:1–18

Galatians 5:1–6

Jude 17–25

'To him who is able to keep you from falling and to present you before his glorious presence without fault and with great joy ...'
Jude 24

F inally we must learn to avoid the performance trap. You may not have come across the expression 'the performance trap' before so let me explain it to you. The performance trap is living out our lives with the idea that we must always do something in order to be accepted by God. Philip Yancey says this: 'Grace sounds a startling note of contradiction … and every day I must pray anew for the ability to hear its message.' If you are anything like me then you will need to remind yourself every day that we are precious to God not because of what we do but because of who we are. That does not mean our service for God is unimportant or that God does not appreciate it. However, the ground of our acceptance is not what we do for Him but what He does for us.

In the fourth and fifth centuries there were two notable Bible teachers. One was named Augustine and the other Pelagius. Augustine believed that salvation was a matter of grace, and that had God not taken the initiative in saving us then we would not be saved. Pelagius took the opposite view and believed that people can take the initial steps towards salvation using their own effort and do not require grace to do so. Augustine, of course, held the right view. Pelagius methodically worked to please God, Augustine rejoiced in the fact that he was 'chosen by grace'.

Eugene Peterson claims that many Christians are Augustinian in theory but Pelagian in practice. In other words, they work to please God rather than rejoicing in the fact that because they are in Christ He is already pleased with them.

Obsessed by grace

In all of us there is this strange sense that we must do something in order to be accepted. It comes, of course, from our carnal nature that is shot through with a desire to earn approval rather than accept it as a matter of grace. Daniel Rowland, a Welsh revivalist, wrote: 'No sooner do we become Christians and accept salvation by grace than there is an impulse in us to earn God's approval, and we set about obsessively trying to please Him by our good works.' Multitudes of Christians do this, and when they do they fall into the performance trap.

Everywhere you look in Paul's writing, as we said earlier, he has something to say about grace. The word 'grace' appears in the first few verses of every one of his letters, and he signs off every letter with the word 'grace'. Grace was the central motif of his life. Transformed on the Damascus Road, he never got over the fact that grace sought him, grace bought him, and grace taught him. Frederick Buechner, the well known American Bible commentator, says of Paul's greetings to his readers: 'Grace is the best he [Paul] can wish them because grace is the best he himself ever received.'

> God loves people because of who He is, not because of what they do.

Paul emphasised grace to such a degree because he knew what would happen to Christians if they responded to the instinct to try and earn God's love. They would become workaholics, driven by the idea that God would stop loving them if they were not being busy. Paul counted himself as the worst of sinners (1 Tim. 1:15), and he knew beyond doubt that God loves people because of who He is, not because of what they do. We simply must get this truth into our heads for if we don't then we will end up working to be saved instead of working because we are saved.

'I am the one Jesus loves'

All commentators agree that when John wrote the phrase – 'the one Jesus loved' (John 20:2) – he was referring to himself. Brennan Manning, author of *The Ragamuffin Gospel*, a book I have come to treasure, said in one of his seminars: 'If John were to be asked, "What is your primary identity in life?" he would not reply, "I am a disciple, an apostle, an evangelist, an author of one of the four Gospels," but rather: "I am the one Jesus loves."' What would it mean for us, I wonder, if we saw ourselves first and foremost not in the roles we play in life – as ministers, car mechanics, nurses, schoolteachers, engineers, shop assistants, and so on – but as 'the one Jesus loves'? I will tell you what it would mean: we would cease trying to impress the Lord by our performance and rejoice in the fact that we are the objects of His affection.

The story is told of an Irish priest who, while walking

through his parish one day, saw an elderly peasant kneeling by the side of the road praying. The priest was impressed at the sight, and quietly going up to the man he remarked: 'You must be very close to God.' The peasant looked up from his prayers, thought for a moment, and said: 'Yes, He's very fond of me.' That peasant was probably closer to God than most because he saw himself as the one who was loved.

We must get it in our hearts that there is nothing we can do to make God love us more. No amount of spiritual discipline, attendance of seminars, study of the Bible in Hebrew and Greek, can make God love us more than He does. He loves us as much as it is possible for an infinite God to love. That's where our true identity must be found – in being loved.

'The tyranny of the oughts'

Now we come to ask ourselves: 'What are some of the signs that Christians are caught up in the performance trap?' The six most common signs are these. First, a never-ending battle with what has been described as the 'tyranny of the oughts' – the feeling that one ought always to be trying hard to please God and, however hard the effort, that one ought always to try harder. Second, an overwhelming sense of guilt and condemnation even when there is no known sin to be repented of. Third, a high degree of anxiety. Fourth, a sense of low esteem from constantly belittling oneself. Fifth, repression of the emotions, and sixth, a spirit of legalism resulting from an oversensitive conscience.

Do you identify with some of these signs? Perhaps you feel like the missionary who once told me: 'I never feel that God is pleased with me unless I am working myself to death, I am weighed down with some sickness, or I am at the point of exhaustion.' This lady was trapped on the treadmill of performance and saw no way of getting off. At the heart of the performance trap is a diabolical lie that our spiritual life depends entirely on how we perform. There were people in the Galatian churches with that outlook. They started out living by grace but fell into the performance trap. What is common to all who fall into the performance trap is the belief that God is not pleased with their efforts.

A child of
His grace.

If I am describing you then settle the issue once and for all: God does not delight in you for what you do but for who you are, a child of His grace. If you never did another hour of service for Him He would not love you less.

Who holds who?

'If you never did another hour of service for Him He would not love you less.' At first that statement might seem dangerous, as it might encourage some to give less to God in terms of their time, talents, and treasure. Not so, however.

Some years ago I talked to a woman who was caught up in the performance trap (doing dutiful things because she believed her acceptance by God depended on this). I said to her: 'I know what I am going to say is not really possible, but suppose you could lie down on this floor and go to sleep for a whole year. When you awoke do you believe God would love you as much as He did when you fell asleep?' She thought for a moment and replied: 'I don't believe so.' 'Why?' I asked. 'Well,' she said, 'I would not have been reading my Bible, attended prayer meetings, given my tithes, not done anything to bring people to Christ …' 'No, I don't think that would make any difference,' I said quietly and firmly. 'This is where you are greatly mistaken. God would love you when you awoke as much as He did when you fell asleep. Nothing in you can extinguish His love, and nothing in you can increase it.' That simple statement seemed to break through her barrier of legalism and she caught such a glimpse of God's unconditional love that in a matter of days she became a transformed person.

A car hire company used to have as its slogan 'We try harder'. The Christian life is not a matter of trying but trusting – trusting that the grace by which we're saved is powerful enough to sustain us also. It is not a case of needing to hold on to God but of letting Him hold us. Never forget that.

Further Study
Exod. 19:1–6; Deut. 7:6–9; John 15:9–17; 1 Pet. 2:4–10
1. What was the foundation of Israel's existence?
2. How does Peter describe the people of God?

1 Kings 19:1–18; Luke 5:1–11; Rom. 8:1–4
3. How did the Lord reassure Elijah?
4. How did Jesus reassure Peter?

*Psa. 139:1–24; Prov. 28:26; 29:25; Isa. 41:8–14; 42:1–9;
1 Pet. 1:1–9*
5. What promises does the Lord make to His servant?
6. In what does Peter want his readers to rejoice?

CHAPTER NINE

AN ALTOGETHER CHRISTIAN

Galatians 4:1–7

Romans 5:12–21

2 Corinthians 9:6–15

'Thanks be to God for his indescribable gift!'
2 Corinthians 9:15

On 24 May 1738 at a quarter to nine in the evening John Wesley, an Anglican clergyman and missionary, sat in a house in Aldersgate in the city of London listening to someone reading from Luther's Preface to the Epistle to Romans. As he heard Luther's description of the change which God works in the heart through faith in Christ he said that he felt his 'heart strangely warmed'. He added: 'I felt I did trust in Christ, Christ alone, for salvation; and an assurance was given me that He had taken away my sins, even mine, and saved me from the law of sin and death.' John Wesley became what he called 'an altogether Christian', and said also that whereas before he had the religion of a servant, after his conversion he had that of a son.

It is true, of course, that we are called God's servants in Scripture, and that must not be denied, but when it comes to describing the relationship as opposed to the role the best word to use is 'son' or 'child'. A servant is appreciated on the basis of what he (or she) does; a child on the basis of who he is. The servant starts out determined to please the master; the child knows he already has his parents' pleasure. The servant is accepted because of his workmanship; the child because of a relationship. When a servant fails, as Dr David Seamands points out, 'his or her whole position is at stake. In a normal home when a child fails or violates the laws of the home he or she may feel grieved that they have blundered or been ineffectual, and will submit themselves to discipline, but they know in their hearts they still belong and are deeply loved.'

Always remember, your role may be that of a servant but your relationship is that of a child.

Superabounding grace

'Most Christians,' says Charles Swindoll, expressing what must be considered a revolutionary thought, 'have been better trained to expect and handle their sin than to expect and enjoy their freedom.' The church in which I was brought up was a legalistic church (it was still a wonderful church, for all that). However, I found that once I began to appreciate that we are not only saved by grace but also sustained by it I gained far more victory over sin than I did in my legalistic days. I shall never forget the moment when the Holy Spirit illuminated the words of Romans 5 verse 20.

If we are free then let's live as if we are.

Though I had read them many times before, on this particular occasion they exploded in my heart. It was as if God said to me: 'You were once enslaved to all kinds of passions but now you are free from that slavery. Where sin abounds, grace superabounds.'

Many Christians begin the day with a fear that they may sin, and end it with a list of things they feel they have to confess. And if one evening the list is not very long they fear they may have overlooked 'hidden sins'. 'Perhaps I have become proud,' they say to themselves. Are freed people supposed to live such a fearful existence? The question we must ask ourselves is this: Are we emancipated or not? If we are free then let's live as if we are. 'So if the Son sets you free,' says Jesus, 'you will be free indeed' (John 8:36).

How much better it is to begin every day with thoughts of victory rather than defeat, to awake to grace not shame, to face every situation in the confidence that we can fail without losing our relationship with our heavenly Father. I assure you that if you walk in the knowledge of that then it will enable you to fail less.

Grace comes with everything

The one thing we need to do above all others to get out of the performance trap is to humbly confess that we have fallen into it. So right now let your mind run over the past few months and years. Have you fallen into the trap of thinking that you must always do something to be accepted by God? Then I have to tell you that underlying that thought is pride. Does that surprise you? You see, pride works not only in downright hostility to God but it is there also when we relegate Him to irrelevance.

If you have come to the point where you are depending more on your own resources to run your life than on the grace God gives then it is time for an act of repentance. Listen to the words of Proverbs 3 verse 34: '[The Lord] mocks proud mockers but gives grace to the humble.' Grace is available for every aspect of the Christian life, and if you have been caught in the performance trap then there is grace flowing towards you now to enable you to repent. And more, much more than you need.

Once I was in Memphis, Tennessee, and went with a friend into a diner for breakfast. I ordered bacon and eggs – just bacon and eggs. However, when my order arrived it came with something called 'grits' – a kind of porridge popular in the deep South. 'But I didn't order grits,' I exclaimed. The waitress replied: 'Maybe you didn't, but at breakfast time grits come with everything.' It's the same with grace. It comes with everything in the Christian life. It is there right now to help you ask God to forgive you for misunderstanding the gospel of free grace and come to the glorious realisation that you don't have to do anything to earn His love. You already have it.

The gift we needed most

We are coming now to the end of our study on the theme of grace. I feel somewhat like the writer to the Hebrews, who said: 'And what more shall I say? I do not have time to tell about Gideon, Barak, Samson, Jephthah, David, Samuel and the prophets' (Heb. 11:32). Clearly he had run out of time but not out of things to say. It is the same with grace. Much has been said, but I assure you more, much more, could be said.

A friend once sent me a Christmas card with these words which impressed me deeply. They form a fitting conclusion to what we have been considering:

If our greatest need had been information,
God would have sent us an educator.
If our greatest need had been technology,
God would have sent us a scientist.
If our greatest need had been money,
God would have sent us an economist.
If our greatest need had been pleasure,
God would have sent us an entertainer.
But our greatest need was forgiveness,
so God sent us a Saviour!

When, on that first Christmas morning, Mary looked at the face of her newborn son, I wonder, did she realise that she was unwrapping for humanity what Paul calls God's indescribable gift? That indescribable gift of grace was the gift we needed most.

It really is amazing
Doesn't it strike you as fascinating that the last word in the Bible is a word about grace? And so it should be, for it is not only the first word in everything but the last word also. Nothing is greater than grace. Nothing! When John Newton wrote his hymn about grace he used the word 'amazing' to describe it. As someone who constantly uses words I have tried to think of a better word to describe it, but there just isn't one. It really is amazing.

Nothing is greater than grace.

Maybe you have seen the documentary made by Bill Moyers on the hymn 'Amazing Grace'. One of the scenes shows Wembley Stadium in London, where several bands had gathered for a rock festival. The concert lasted for twelve hours, and you can imagine the mood of the crowd by the end of that time, many of them high on drink and drugs. The festival concluded with a song from an opera singer by the name of Jessye Norman – a beautiful African American woman. She chose as her song 'Amazing Grace'. Without any accompaniment she began to sing slowly:

Amazing grace! how sweet the sound,
That saved a wretch like me!
I once was lost, but now I'm found;
Was blind, but now I see.

By the time she reached the last verse a strange power had descended on the stadium. All was quiet.

Non-Christians as well as Christians are amazed by grace. Though they may not realise it, that is what they thirst for. And when it is seen – not just sung – then all the world will fall silent before it. It's amazing. Utterly amazing.

Further Study

Exod. 4:18–23; Hosea 11:1–11; Luke 15:11–32;
1 John 3:1–3
1. In what terms did Hosea express God's love for Israel?
2. Why did the father celebrate in the parable Jesus told?

Psa. 147:1–20; 149:1–4; 1 Cor. 13:4–7; Eph. 3:12–21
3. For what does the psalmist give praise?
4. In what did Paul place his confidence?

Psa. 67:1–7; 111:1–10; 2 Cor. 13:14; Eph. 6:23;
1 Tim. 1:15–17; 2:1–6
5. Extol the Lord, with the psalmist.
6. How did Paul respond to God's mercy?

NATIONAL DISTRIBUTORS

UK: (and countries not listed below)
CWR, Waverley Abbey House, Waverley Lane, Farnham, Surrey GU9 8EP.
Tel: (01252) 784700 Outside UK +44 1252 784700

AUSTRALIA: CMC Australasia, PO Box 519, Belmont, Victoria 3216.
Tel: (03) 5241 3288

CANADA: Cook Communications Ministries, PO Box 98, 55 Woodslee
Avenue, Paris, Ontario. Tel: 1800 263 2664

GHANA: Challenge Enterprises of Ghana, PO Box 5723, Accra.
Tel: (021) 222437/223249 Fax: (021) 226227

HONG KONG: Cross Communications Ltd, 1/F, 562A Nathan Road,
Kowloon. Tel: 2780 1188 Fax: 2770 6229

INDIA: Crystal Communications, 10-3-18/4/1, East Marredpalli,
Secunderabad – 500026, Andhra Pradesh. Tel/Fax: (040) 27737145

KENYA: Keswick Books and Gifts Ltd, PO Box 10242, Nairobi.
Tel: (02) 331692/226047 Fax: (02) 728557

MALAYSIA: Salvation Book Centre (M) Sdn Bhd, 23 Jalan SS 2/64, 47300
Petaling Jaya, Selangor. Tel: (03) 78766411/78766797
Fax: (03) 78757066/78756360

NEW ZEALAND: CMC Australasia, PO Box 36015, Lower Hutt.
Tel: 0800 449 408 Fax: 0800 449 049

NIGERIA: FBFM, Helen Baugh House, 96 St Finbarr's College Road, Akoka,
Lagos. Tel: (01) 7747429/4700218/825775/827264

PHILIPPINES: OMF Literature Inc, 776 Boni Avenue, Mandaluyong City.
Tel: (02) 531 2183 Fax: (02) 531 1960

SINGAPORE: Armour Publishing Pte Ltd, Block 203A Henderson Road,
11–06 Henderson Industrial Park, Singapore 159546. Tel: 6 276 9976
Fax: 6 276 7564

SOUTH AFRICA: Struik Christian Books, 80 MacKenzie Street, PO Box
1144, Cape Town 8000. Tel: (021) 462 4360 Fax: (021) 461 3612

SRI LANKA: Christombu Books, 27 Hospital Street, Colombo 1.
Tel: (01) 433142/328909

TANZANIA: CLC Christian Book Centre, PO Box 1384, Mkwepu Street,
Dar es Salaam. Tel/Fax: (022) 2119439

USA: Cook Communications Ministries, PO Box 98, 55 Woodslee Avenue,
Paris, Ontario, Canada. Tel: 1800 263 2664

ZIMBABWE: Word of Life Books, Shop 4, Memorial Building, 35 S Machel
Avenue, Harare. Tel: (04) 781305 Fax: (04) 774739

For email addresses, visit the CWR website: www.cwr.org.uk

CWR is a registered charity – number 294387

Day and Residential Courses
Counselling Training
Leadership Development
Biblical Study Courses
Regional Seminars
Ministry to Women
Daily Devotionals
Books and Videos
Conference Centre

Trusted all Over the World

CWR HAS GAINED A WORLDWIDE reputation as a centre of excellence for Bible-based training and resources. From our headquarters at Waverley Abbey House, Farnham, England, we have been serving God's people for 40 years with a vision to help apply God's Word to everyday life and relationships. The daily devotional *Every Day with Jesus* is read by nearly a million readers an issue in more than 150 countries, and our unique courses in biblical studies and pastoral care are respected all over the world. Waverley Abbey House provides a conference centre in a tranquil setting.

For free brochures on our seminars and courses, conference facilities, or a catalogue of CWR resources, please contact us at the following address.
CWR, Waverley Abbey House, Waverley Lane, Farnham, Surrey GU9 8EP, UK

Telephone: +44 (0)1252 784700
Email: mail@cwr.org.uk
Website: www.cwr.org.uk

CWR CRUSADE FOR WORLD REVIVAL
Applying God's Word to everyday life and relationships

Prayer – A Fresh Vision

This book will encourage you to take a fresh look at
your prayer life and teach you how to offer effective
prayers that touch the heart of God and keep you in
His will. Don't miss talking with your Father in
heaven; learn the essentials of effective prayer:
worship and adoration, thanksgiving and praise,
petition and intercession, listening and confession.

£6.99 (plus p&p)
ISBN: 1-85345-308-0

The Holy Spirit, Our Counsellor

Focusing on the Holy Spirit, 'the Counsellor' who will never leave us, Selwyn writes of His role in our lives. He compares His counselling with that of Christ. The Holy Spirit lives in us and brings transformation. A book to encourage us to go straight to Him for our 'counselling' needs as we are reminded to open ourselves to the power and working of the Holy Spirit.

£6.99 (plus p&p)

ISBN: 1-85345-309-9